A PONY CLUB PU

CH00767747

Choosin ◡
Buying a Pony

CUMBRIA COUNTY
WITHDRAWN
FROM
STOCK
LIBRARIES

Che

Fetl

A PONY CLUB PUBLICATION

Choosing and Buying a Pony

THE BRITISH HORSE SOCIETY
and **THE PONY CLUB**

© The British Horse Society 1990

Text by Toni Webber
Illustrations by Ann Woodrow
Endpapers taken from *The Manual of Horsemanship*, 9th Edition
Photographs by Shona Wood, *Pony Magazine*, Trevor Meeks and John Birt
Cover photographs by Sally Anne Thompson, Animal Photography and
David Blunt

All rights reserved. No part of this publication may be reproduced, stored in
a retrieval system, or transmitted, in any form or by any means, electronic,
mechanical, photocopying, recording or otherwise, without the prior permission of The Pony Club.

Published by The Pony Club

Designed and produced by
The Kenilworth Press Limited,
661 Fulham Road, London SW6 5PZ

Typeset by DMD

Printed in Great Britain by Hollen Street Press

British Library Cataloguing in Publication Data
Choosing and buying a pony.
   1. Livestock: Ponies
   I. Pony club
   636.16

   ISBN 0–900226–38–2

Contents

Introduction

Buying a pony for the first time is very exciting. It can also be quite daunting and, if you make a mistake, expensive to put right. But the parents of most of the children you see riding around were first-time buyers themselves at one time and neither they nor their offspring appear to rue the day they entered into pony-ownership. So there is no reason why you should not join them.

The secret lies in careful preparation. You must know why you want to buy a pony, where to go to find one and how to tell if he is the right one for you once you have found him.

This book is intended to guide you through the pitfalls. It cannot guarantee that the pony you finally settle for will be absolutely perfect but it should help you to avoid making dreadful mistakes.

You may even find perfection. After all, ask any rider to name the most wonderful pony in the world and the chances are that they will point to the one they are riding. So there must be a lot of perfect ponies around.

ABOVE: Riding should, above all, be fun for both child and pony. These two nice ponies seem to be enjoying jumping as much as their young riders.

BELOW: If you want to make the games team, choose a calm, willing pony which leads well. This one looks to have good all-round qualities.

1

Planning to Buy

Ponies change hands through advertisements, dealers, sale-rings, recommendation and, occasionally, via rescue agencies. If you are fortunate, the first pony that you look at will be just the one you want; on the other hand, you could spend many months examining and rejecting ponies before you find the one which most closely fits your requirements. And even then, there may be drawbacks.

For the first-time pony-owner it is difficult to know how to draw up the specification for an ideal pony.

To begin with, you should look at the advantages and disadvantages of owning a pony. After you have taken the first step of deciding to buy one, it is only too easy to forget to do your homework properly.

ADVANTAGES OF OWNING A PONY

- The pony is available when you want him, to ride where you like and when you like.
- You can build up an understanding with him: a relationship which is difficult to achieve when you ride, say, once a week and when other riders are using the pony.
- You have the chance to make lasting friendships with other pony-owners in your area.
- You have a living creature of your very own on whom to lavish love and affection.
- With care – and correct training – your pony could be an appreciating asset, worth more when you come to sell him than you had to pay for him.

DISADVANTAGES OF OWNING A PONY
- The pony's welfare is your responsibility. He must be fed, watered and exercised every day even when you are feeling ill or when the weather is foul.
- He is a commitment. If you decide that you want to give up riding and take up hang-gliding or wind-surfing, you cannot just stow the pony away in a cupboard or the attic; you must find him another home.
- He is a continuing expense. Although the annual costs of keeping a pony can be roughly calculated, your budget should always allow for the unexpected.

Most people learn to ride at a riding school. At some schools you may be required to tack up and untack the pony at the beginning and end of your lesson, but in many cases you get on to the pony as soon as the previous pupil has dismounted.

For the hour or so of your ride, the pony will be repeating most of the actions he carried out at the earlier lesson. Although you will believe that it is from the way in which you apply the aids that the pony will know what to do next, he will actually soon learn what is expected of him and will walk, trot, canter and jump at the same time and in the same way every hour.

Instructors know how long each phase of a lesson takes and what most pupils expect for their money. You may occasionally vary the proceedings by hacking out, but even then a nice circular tour which lasts about three-quarters of an hour and gives every pupil a short spell of cantering and a calm walk home is unlikely to be varied to any degree. No wonder the competent pupils begin to want more variety in their equestrian lives!

It is at this stage that a rider thinks of buying a pony.

Every prospective owner should now start taking a serious look at the options. In general, this means answering the following questions:
- Where am I going to keep the pony?
- How much time can I spare to take care of him?

- How much per week, or month, or year, can I afford to spend on a pony's upkeep?
- How much capital can I lay out on a pony and on the equipment he will need?
- Who will look after him when I am away or ill?

Only when all the answers are satisfactory can you then decide what sort of pony to buy.

If you are a child or, at least, a non-earner, you must sit down with your parents and discuss the prospect seriously. Some children have parents who ride themselves; others have parents – usually their mother – who used to ride, maybe even owned a pony, and quite like the idea of doing so again; many children have parents who know nothing at all about horses. All parents, however, must have one thing in common – they should feel completely happy at the prospect of their son or daughter owning a pony and be willing to help both financially and with encouragement. Whatever you may read in fiction, it is almost impossible for a child to pay for the upkeep of a pony out of earnings from a paper-round or cleaning the neighbour's car.

KEEPING A PONY

Most ponies of 14.2hh (hands high) or under can live out all the year round. A stable is not necessary unless the pony is sick, but it is useful to have one available for, say, the night before a show or if in exceptionally wet weather the pasture becomes waterlogged.

Living out means occupying a field or fields of adequate size, with safe fences and gates, a constant supply of clean, fresh water, some form of shelter or windbreak and, preferably, companions. One pony needs at least two acres to provide him with sufficient grass during the summer. He also needs supplementary rations of dried grass (hay) during the winter. These are the minimum requirements, though

11

with careful pasture management two ponies could manage on three acres.

It is thus obvious that a back garden is not a suitable place for keeping a pony in. Even a small orchard may not be big enough. If, therefore, you have no land of your own which is suitable for a pony you must make arrangements to rent a field.

Landowners prepared to lease out their fields for horses usually do so in one of two ways: they will offer a grass or grazing lease or they will charge you a weekly rent for keeping your pony in their field. Of the two systems, the latter is the more expensive.

Grazing lease

Most grazing contracts are issued for one year at a time. Usually they are renewable, although the rent may be altered at the time of renewal. The contract may stipulate that the lessee (you) is responsible for the fencing and the provision of water. Fencing of an agreed standard may also be stipulated.

The advantage of obtaining grazing rights is that you can put another pony in the field without having to pay additional rent. A five-acre field, for example, could support three ponies and, under a grazing tenancy, cost just the same as if there were only one.

This type of lease, however, is not always easy to come by.

Weekly rent

A much more common arrangement is to be charged for the use of a field per pony per week. Any additional ponies are charged at the same amount, so that your weekly rent will double or treble if you become ambitious and decide to have more than one pony of your own to ride and compete on. If you arrange for your friend to keep a pony with yours (and to pay the same rent as yourself) it is very important for any written agreement with your landlord to be in your name and to give you jurisdiction over how many ponies may use the field and who owns them. You never want to find yourself in a situation where your landlord can invite other people to keep their ponies with yours.

Where the weekly charge is per pony, the landlord is usually responsible for the water supply and for keeping the fences and gates in good order.

Livery
There is a third option for the landless owner to keep a pony, and that is to put him at livery.

A livery yard is one where several owners keep their animals and pay weekly or monthly fees for whatever facilities or services are available. The charges will be quite high and will vary according to the amount of responsibility that the livery yard has to undertake.

FULL LIVERY
In a full livery, the yard owner agrees to look after your pony at all times: feeding him, overseeing his shoeing and carrying out a vaccination and worming programme as necessary. Apart from the yard assistants, no one will ride the pony except yourself and he will be available for your use whenever you want him. Not surprisingly, since you are handing over the complete care of your pony to someone else, full livery charges are very high.

PART-LIVERY
Lower down the scale is the part-livery. In this case you share the responsibility of your pony with the livery yard, paying separately or by separate arrangement for his food and undertaking to do such things as muck out his stable (if he is coming in at night) and exercising him mainly yourself.

For many owners, especially those who have a demanding job, this is an ideal arrangement. They may be able to get away from work at lunchtime and are happy to muck out the stable, but because of morning and evening commitments may prefer the yard owners to turn the pony out and bring him in at night. If they are away for any reason – on business or on holiday – the yard will take on the care of the pony at no extra cost.

DIY-LIVERY
The cheapest livery of all is the do-it-yourself livery. This is similar to renting a field – because you are totally responsible for the pony's welfare – but it has three particular advantages: (1) that there are other ponies around to keep yours company; (2) that you can usually arrange – perhaps at extra cost – for someone to care for him when you are on holiday; and (3) that you have free use of whatever facilities the livery yard provides for its clients: cross-country course, all-weather school, show jumps, etc.

If you do decide to keep your new pony at livery, make certain that you choose a reputable yard. There are unscrupulous livery yards, often charging high prices, where ponies are turned out all together and not inspected regularly; where mares and geldings are mixed up and no one checks to see whether there has been any kicking; where horses are stabled without water, or poor quality food is given; and where other people's ponies are ridden indiscriminately by anyone looking for a ride.

WORKING LIVERY
Riding schools sometimes offer to look after a pony in return for using him in the school. This can work very well, especially if you have bought the pony from the school in the first place or if your pony is definitely a beginners' mount, but beware of making such an arrangement with a young or flighty pony or one which has tremendous competitive potential. The routine and often boring work of a riding school pony can have a deadening effect on his character.

PRIVATE LIVERY
The very best arrangement is to be able to keep your pony with a close friend, who not only rides but who has a pony and sufficient land to keep both ponies. It is unlikely that your friend's parents will charge you a high rent and,

provided that you pay for the food your pony eats and do your fair share of the work, you and your friend will have a wonderful few years of pleasure and close companionship.

CALCULATING THE COSTS
Do not rush out to buy a pony until you have worked out exactly what the costs of keeping him are likely to be.

CAPITAL OUTLAY

Cost of pony This can vary from a few hundred to several thousand pounds, depending on the past history of the pony. An older pony, totally safe in all circumstances but not necessarily highly competitive (in other words, the ideal first pony), is at the lower end of the price range. A competitive pony which has qualified for or won major championships will be expensive. In between are the good all-rounders, the ponies who have been used for many different Pony Club activities and perhaps have an excellent local reputation but who are not in fact top class.

Cost of equipment This covers the essentials – saddle, bridle, headcollar, lead-rope, bandages, etc., as well as such items as grooming kit, buckets, feed bowl and other items that no self-respecting pony can do without. Many items, however, can be acquired in stages and many make excellent birthday and Christmas presents in the years to come.

Freeze-branding Theft of horses is an ever-present problem, and the most effective deterrent is the brand-mark. Branding is carried out by an expert working for a central agency which allocates an individual number to your pony. The number is literally frozen on, and though the process may tickle a little, it is otherwise painless. At first a scab forms and then, after about 12 weeks, new white hairs grow through, leaving the pony indelibly stamped with his number. The number is registered with the agency.

Whatever the reason for the theft – whether the animal is intended to end up in the meat-market or for private sale – the freeze-mark provides instant identification and no abattoir or private buyer would buy a pony without the relevant papers to establish legal ownership.

Freeze-marking is fairly cheap, and the cost can be further reduced if the operator can brand several ponies at one visit. Many Pony Club branches organise freeze-marking sessions to enable members to take advantage of the bulk rate.

The mark can be placed anywhere on the pony's body. Many owners choose to have it under the saddle, where it will be hidden when the pony is being ridden, but the shoulder and quarters are also popular areas.

If you buy a pony which has already been freeze-marked all you will have to pay the agency is the cost of transferring the pony to your name.

MAINTENANCE COSTS

Field or livery rent　If you have your own field, this will cost you nothing. Rents, however, usually start at around £5 per week and can reach £75 to £100 weekly for a good livery yard. Always make enquiries locally to find out what the going rate in your neighbourhood happens to be.

Food　Contrary to the layman's expectations, a pony being ridden regularly cannot live solely on grass. In summer, it is true, a grass-kept pony can keep healthy on grass alone, but in winter, when the grass has little nutritional value, extra food will be required. This means paying for hay. Good-quality meadow hay is best for small ponies; good quality seed hay for bigger ones. If your pony has any kind of respiratory problem, it may be necessary to buy vacuum-packed haylage, which is dust and spore-free but also expensive. Do not imagine that you can save money by buying cheap hay – it will almost certainly cause harm to your pony in the long run.

As well as hay, the pony will require other forms of food,

especially if you are taking part in regular activities and competitions. In winter, he will need body-building food such as soaked sugar beet or cooked barley, together with chaff to improve his digestive processes. He may need compound foods, such as cubes or mixes, or oats to give him energy.

All these foods are costly and, although they work out cheaper if bought in bulk, you need sufficient long-term storage for items such as hay, and it is not wise to bulk-buy foods which have a limited shelf life – oats, barley, etc.

Worming All ponies have parasites which live in their gut. Provided there are not too many of them, they do not do the animals any harm. However, it is very easy for ponies to become badly infested by worms from poorly managed and over-grazed pastures, and their health will then suffer. All pony-owners should carry out regular worming procedures. There are a number of pastes and powders on the market. They are not expensive and your budget should include an allowance for worming doses to be given every eight to twelve weeks; more often if your pony is kept on pasture that has to maintain many other ponies.

Fields which are regularly rotated, so that one or more is left fallow or used for a hay crop, are less likely to become severely contaminated. If the rotation system also includes periods of grazing by sheep or cattle, the pasture will be even better because horse worms cannot survive in the gut of sheep and cattle and will die. It is possible to have a worm count analysis made of the soil.

Where rotation is not possible, the horse droppings should be collected daily and removed.

Vaccination It is possible to protect your pony against tetanus and equine influenza by arranging for him to be vaccinated regularly. Tetanus, or lockjaw, is particularly dangerous, but an initial course followed by an annual booster will give the pony complete protection. Equine 'flu is not usually fatal but would keep your pony off work for several weeks. It is very infectious and there are many

17

establishments, such as racecourses and riding schools, which will not allow ponies on to the property unless they have a valid certificate of vaccination. As with tetanus, an initial course is followed by an annual booster and the two vaccines can be given in one dose. Your budget should allow for the cost of the vaccine and the vet's visit, as well as a vaccination certificate, popularly known as the pony's 'passport'.

Shoeing Most ponies need shoes to protect their hooves from splitting. If your pony has strong hooves and you rarely ride on hard surfaces, it is possible to leave him unshod, but he will still need regular visits from the farrier to keep his feet in trim. Ponies wear out shoes at different rates and sometimes their feet need trimming although the shoes are still serviceable. In this case, the farrier will replace the old shoes after tidying up the feet.

Always find out by asking around who is the best farrier in your area. He may not be the cheapest but it is worth spending extra to have your pony's feet well cared for. Expect to have to call him out every eight weeks or so, although some ponies may need shoeing more often.

Pony Club membership This is an annual cost which will really enhance your pleasure in owning a pony. Apart from being able to obtain advice on any problems that you may be having with your pony, you will be given free riding and horsecare instruction, have the opportunity to take part in Pony Club competitions and team events, go with your pony to an annual camp and, best of all, make many new pony-loving friends.

Show entries Do not forget to allow several pounds in your budget for show entries. Once you have a pony, you are certain to want to take part in local shows, gymkhanas, hunter trials and one-day events, and entry fees soon mount up. Even if you are good enough to win or to be placed in a show, prize money is never awarded in Pony Club competitions; and even when local shows offer money prizes, the winnings are unlikely to cover your expenses. You should, however, soon start to acquire numerous rosettes which are great souvenirs but have no intrinsic value.

Travelling expenses   These should not be very great to start with, but they tend to increase as you become more ambitious. Unless you can make an arrangement with a friend who has a trailer, you will have to hire transport to reach shows that are too far away to hack to. You will also have to get to training sessions if you join, for example, your Pony Club branch's mounted games squad.

Sooner or later, you will no doubt want a trailer of your own. A good secondhand one will cost £1000 or more. This, of course, should really go under your list of capital expenditure, but most new pony-owners start by hiring.

Veterinary costs   Apart from the annual vaccination, you could be lucky with your pony and not need to call the vet out at all. But accidents can happen, however careful you may be, and you should be aware that veterinary treatment can be quite expensive.

Insurance   Premiums are based on the value of the pony and the type of riding activity. You can buy extra cover for your tack, veterinary costs, loss of use and a few other items. Always shop around for the policy which gives the best value for money and remember that premiums may be reduced if your pony has been freeze-marked. Most policies contain exclusion clauses, and you should always read the small print carefully.

Membership of the Pony Club automatically offers legal personal liability cover to the member. This comes under the Pony Club section of the British Horse Society's policy of insurance, which is held at headquarters and can be inspected if required.

2

Identifying Your Requirements

Two of the most important factors in selecting a particular pony are your own riding ability and what you expect to do when you have him.

RIDING ABILITY

Your riding ability partly depends on the stage that you have reached at your riding school. Most new pony-owners are capable of riding off the leading rein and may also have learned to jump before they consider getting a pony of their own. A few, very novice young riders acquire their own pony whilst they are still at the leading-rein stage, but in this case there are usually knowledgeable parents in the background prepared to take full responsibility for the pony's welfare.

You must be honest about yourself. Even at quite a young age, a child's individual characteristics are apparent. You do not have to be gutsy, ambitious or totally fearless to get a great deal of pleasure out of owning and riding a pony. These traits are useful if you plan to compete at Badminton but the vast majority of riders are quite content to spend their time in quiet hacking or taking part in small, friendly, local competitions.

So you must make an objective assessment of your temperament and – even more important – make certain that your parents understand your temperament as well.

Are you nervous?

Most people suffer from some form of nervousness when they first start to ride. If you are to find the right pony for you, you must analyse your nerves and decide what causes them.

Fear of the unknown

Solution Familiarity and practice will soon make the fear disappear, so do not expect to achieve complete confidence in your pony until you have been looking after and riding him for six months or more.

Physical fear Perhaps of the pony bolting, plunging or rearing, thus causing you to fall off.

Solution Any pony that you ride will sense your feelings and will become nervous himself, which only makes the matter worse. You should therefore choose a pony with a stolid temperament, one who is described as capable of taking care of his rider. An older pony, which has been around a long time and knows the ropes, could be the best choice for you.

Fear when handling the pony from the ground

Solution You need a pony with a kind and gentle manner, one which never objects to having his feet picked up, his ears touched or his mane and tail pulled. This pony rarely puts his ears back or nips.

Fear of losing control

Solution A forward-going pony will only make the feeling worse. Choose a pony which, if anything, needs pushing on.

Are you ambitious?

Ambition is a driving force, but it can take many forms. It is important to decide how ambitious you really are and to tailor your choice of pony accordingly.

Identifying Your Requirements

Determined to make a name for yourself

Solution   No one can predict the future, but you can make a good start by looking for a ready-made pony who has already gained a reputation in the type of competition you enjoy. You will have to pay more for such a pony and to consolidate your partnership with him by taking lessons from a leading instructor and giving up other interests.

Fairly competitive

Solution   Most riders find competitions fun and take part mainly for that reason. Winning a rosette, however, is a thrill, and for that you need a pony capable of performing well, provided that the standard is not too high.

Not competitive at all

Solution   If you are simply not interested in pitting your skill at riding against others and would prefer light hacking, there is no need for you to look for a pony with a reputation for doing well in competitions. However, the seller of such a pony usually hopes to find a buyer with some ambition and may feel that the pony would be wasted if he were sold to you.

The right assessment
When analysing your character, the most difficult task is to persuade your parents that your assessment of yourself is the correct one. Many people have been put off riding for life by parents who are over-ambitious for their offspring. It is natural for a mother or father to speak with pride of a successful child and to enjoy receiving the congratulations, however insincere, from other parents when the child takes a valued trophy or makes the first team at a young age. **But no parents should ever allow their own vicarious ambitions to supersede the well-being and confidence of the child.**

WHAT A PONY IS EXPECTED TO DO

First pony

A pony suitable for beginners is quiet, willing, easy to handle and responsive to his rider's wishes. He does not have to be very fast nor to be able to jump well but he should be capable of tackling a small jumping course without ever refusing or running out. His paces should be even and he should not 'lean' on the rider's hands, nor make a beeline for the nearest patch of grass and refuse to move.

Traffic of all kinds should hold no terrors for him and he must be unaffected by loud bangs, fluttering paper, strange objects and other ponies moving away from him.

He should not put his ears back when approached nor snatch at titbits. He must be easy to catch and quiet when being groomed or tacked up.

He should lead willingly whether from another horse or by a handler on foot.

He should do well on comparatively little exercise and be happy, if necessary, to plod along at a walk.

He will inspire great love but his rider, before long, will be looking for a pony with more zip.

Specialist performer

Many ponies are trained specially for one particular activity. This can range from mounted games to cross-country competitions. It does not mean that they are incapable of performing a number of activities but they are often best at one.

If you are determined to make the A team in your Pony Club's mounted games squad, it makes sense to buy a good games pony. But the same pony may not help you if you decide to take up dressage or are looking for success in Pony Club eventing.

All-rounder

The best kind of Pony Club pony is one who is capable of carrying out many different activities. There are, in fact, plenty of ponies around who seem to enjoy everything that they are asked to do. At junior level, they will compete happily in a horse trials one week, a games competition the next, indoor show jumping the week after and, in between, will attend working rallies, take part in polo training and complete a long-distance sponsored ride.

For first-time pony-owners, competent at all paces, this is the ideal pony to look for. Until you have a chance to try different disciplines, you may have no idea of the ones you like best. A good all-rounder will build up your confidence and last you two to three seasons.

MOVING ON

Those who ride at riding schools once a week often have difficulty in judging their own ability. Even if you switch from one pony to another and take part in all the events the riding school arranges, you may be limited in your choice of activities.

It is quite possible that once you have a pony of your own you will discover that you hate going across country and jumping fixed fences but enjoy the discipline and precision of an indoor show-jumping course. You may dislike jumping altogether but find a fascination in the precise art of dressage. You may get your thrills from polo or horseball or discover long-distance riding.

The great advantage of belonging to the Pony Club is that it gives you a chance to try a number of different disciplines. This was not always the case.

Thirty years ago, the average Pony Club member had very little opportunity to take part in competitions that reflected the ability of both rider and pony. A few branches had excellent facilities, generous supporters and enough adults with the time and enthusiasm to take on the training of the young members and their ponies. But most confined their activities to those which were easy to arrange – gymkhanas (out of which grew the mounted games) and show jumping which only needed a field and a few borrowed jumps.

Today, the range of activities is forever widening. Farmers

who ride themselves or have children who ride seem increasingly willing to build a cross-country course across their land; polo enthusiasts turn up trumps with the offer of a large flat field; all-weather schooling areas spring up in corners of smallholdings; and Pony Club parents can be overheard earnestly discussing such details as drainage, membranes and whether sand is better than bark or vice versa.

The result has been an enormous expansion in competitions suitable for all ages, and competitors who seem to get younger every year. There are five-year-olds barely able to lift the gun in tetrathlon, six-year-olds in back numbers which seem to swallow them up riding with great verve over a two-foot cross-country course, and seven-year-olds poring over their dressage sheets and showing every sign of knowing what 'behind the bit' or 'fell into canter' actually mean.

With all this, it is almost inevitable that pony-owners are going to change ponies regularly. Some children seem to acquire a new pony every season; others move on every two years. It is becoming increasingly rare for a pony to stay with one rider for three years or more.

Moving on, however, brings its own problems, and all pony-owners should be aware of them.

The next pony is not just going to be a bigger, more skilful version of the first. Every pony is different in character and temperament: every pony needs to be ridden slightly differently from the one before.

Never forget that it can take up to a year for you and your new pony to become a team.

This is one of the reasons why a pony which won competition after competition last season with his previous owner suddenly hits a losing streak when you are in the saddle. It is very difficult for inexperienced pony-owners to accept this and to realise that time, patience and hard work will pay off in the end. It is particularly difficult when the pony is known to the local riding community and you are well aware that they are comparing your riding unfavourably with the previous owner's.

There are all sorts of things to learn about a new pony which cannot be assessed until the pony has been yours for some time. Some ponies, for example, are more skilled than others at picking the right moment for take-off when going over a jump. These clever ponies will put in an extra stride if they think they need it so that all the rider has to do is to point the pony in the right direction. The next pony may need help from his rider.

Some ponies perform better 'cold', needing little or no warming-up before a dressage test or a show-jumping round. Others need an hour or more to be 'worked in'. If you have been accustomed to arriving at the showground ten minutes before you are due in the ring, it will come as a great shock and disappointment when you try the same tactics with the next pony; and, of course, the other way around.

With the new pony, you may have to change your riding style – sit deeper in the saddle, for instance, or ride with a lighter touch on the reins. It is always worthwhile arranging to have a few private lessons, preferably with a Pony Club instructor, to get advice and to follow it.

Above all, do not be disheartened too easily.

Nevertheless, it is possible to make a mistake in your choice of pony. Some ponies and riders never do manage to establish a relationship. If you are a nervous rider and your new pony has habits which make you more nervous – if he plunges or pulls and you are not a very firm or dominating rider, you will never be able to assert your authority sufficiently to cure him. You can take all the advice and instruction in the world and the situation will never improve because you and your pony are temperamentally unsuited.

In this case, you must be prepared to recognise the situation and to let the pony go to a rider who is right for him. There is no shame in this. It is better to sell the pony on and to continue to search for one who is right for you.

3

Where to Find a Pony

Ponies are sold through advertisements, by word of mouth, via dealers and at auction sales. None of these methods can guarantee that you will find the perfect pony, but for inexperienced buyers the sale-ring is the riskiest and word-of-mouth recommendation is probably the best.

ADVERTISEMENTS

Most equestrian magazines carry advertisements for ponies and horses of all sizes and ability. The most popular magazine for this purpose is **Horse and Hound**, a weekly which is sold nationwide and often bought for its advertisements alone. However, although you will almost certainly find details of a pony which fits your specification somewhere in its pages, you will be very lucky if the vendors live within easy reach of your home.

If travelling is likely to be a problem, you should concentrate your attention first on local papers, especially give-away advertising publications which seem to exist in most areas. These local 'freebies' often have a section devoted entirely to horses, and many good ponies change hands without ever being advertised more widely.

Wording

A glance at any horsey advertisement quickly demonstrates that three lines of small type can be used to great effect in selling a pony. Most advertisers use an established 'shorthand', and before you rush to the telephone you should have some idea of what it all means.

The following terms are in common use:

'Bombproof'   Usually refers to the pony's behaviour in traffic. It can generally be relied upon to mean that the pony is not going to be frightened by any type of vehicle that he meets on the road. Whether this is through common sense or because he is too dispirited to react in any other way is something you will have to find out for yourself.

'Forward-going'   On the positive side, this means that the pony is keen and enjoys his work, and that you will not have to keep kicking him to make him canter. It is up to you to find out whether you can stop him.

'Not a novice ride'   A lively pony with plenty of go – or one who plunges, rears, generally misbehaves or is totally uncontrollable. Take your pick.

'First pony'   A well-mannered pony who takes care of his rider or one who cannot manage anything faster than a walk.

'Schoolmaster'   Usually an experienced, and therefore older, pony who may well be a great asset to an inexperienced rider. But he might also be stubborn, and determined to have his own way.

'Quiet to handle'   This should mean that the pony is well mannered both in and out of the stable, allowing his feet to be picked up or his head to be groomed. It does not guarantee that he is quiet to ride.

'Easy to catch/box/shoe'   Usually a fairly accurate description of a pony's behaviour in the field, trailer, or with the farrier. It is what is left out that is important.

'Always in the ribbons'   Is usually placed in competitions. Check the standard of competition and how often he takes part.

'Never stops'   Refers to the pony's jumping ability, not to his reaction to the rider's commands. However, it may mean that he completes a jumping course as though the jumps were not there. The cleverest jumping pony may put in a stop if he feels he is completely wrong at a jump.

'Loves jumping'   This pony may be a brilliant jumper. It may also mean that, at the sight of a show jump, the pony takes off, regardless of how prepared the rider is.

'Scopey'   Can mean capable of a big jump, or that the pony has potential. If you are a novice, make sure that the jump is not so big that the rider is jumped out of the saddle.

'Snaffle mouth'   This should mean that the pony goes well in a snaffle bit. Some ponies, however, can be ridden in a snaffle only in the confines of a school.

Abbreviations
Advertisements are costly and the more that can be crammed into a small space the better. Abbreviations are very popular and their use is sensible as long as the prospective buyer knows what they mean. Here are some of the most common:

BSJA	British Show Jumping Association.
BSPS	British Show Pony Society.
Ch.	Champion.
CT	Combined Training (dressage and show jumping).
FH	Foxhunter (novice show-jumping competitions).
FR	First ridden (class of working hunter pony for very young riders).

HIS	Hunter Improvement Society.
HOYS	Horse of the Year Show.
HT	Hunter Trials.
ID	Irish Draught (usually in reference to cross-breeding: the product of an Irish Draught and Thoroughbred parents often makes a good jumper).
JA	Top grading for show-jumping ponies in BSJA competitions.
JC	Points grading for registered show-jumping ponies in BSJA competitions.
LR	Leading rein.
LDR	Leading rein.
M&M	Mountain and Moorland.
MGAGB	Mounted Games Association of Great Britain.
NPS	National Pony Society.
ODE	One-day event.
PBA	Ponies of Britain Association.
PC	Pony Club.
PoB	Ponies of Britain.
Pot.	Potential.
PPC	Prince Philip Cup (mounted games).
R&D	Ride and Drive.
RC	Riding Club.
SHP	Show pony of hunter-type.
SJ	Show jumping.
SP	Show pony.
TB	Thoroughbred.
TBX	Crossbred, partly Thoroughbred.
WH	Working hunter.
WHP	Working hunter pony.
XC	Cross-country.
3D or 3DE	Three-day event.

When you have found a likely-sounding pony in the right price bracket you should telephone the vendors and arrange for a viewing. Very few advertisements these days carry a box number and the initial contact is usually made by telephone.

Elicit as many details as you can on the telephone to save wasting both your time and the owner's. If there is anything in the advertisement which you do not understand, ask for clarification. Starting on page 60 is a checklist of questions to put to the owner when inspecting the pony. Some could usefully be asked over the telephone. Make notes and take them with you if you view the pony – and check that you get the same story. As long as the answers are satisfactory, you can go ahead and arrange your visit.

Ask for the name and full address of the vendors, including directions on how to find their house (or stables if the pony is not kept at home). Try to arrange a specific time.

It is important to arrive at the appointed time, and even more important to let the owners know if for any reason you have to cancel your visit. Although you may have allowed yourself all day to try out the pony, the owners may well lead busy lives and may not want to have to hang about waiting for the prospective buyer to turn up.

If possible – especially if your knowledge of ponies is limited – try to take an expert with you. The expert need not necessarily be a qualified instructor but should have had experience of caring for ponies and be sufficiently familiar with your riding ability to know whether the pony is likely to suit you or not.

WORD OF MOUTH

Many good ponies change hands without ever being advertised. They are passed down the family and then on to buyers in the same village or to the same Pony Club branch. The new owner is familiar with the pony, perhaps having had a chance to ride him in the past; the old owners know the type of home to which he is going and the ability of the rider who will be taking him on.

This method of acquiring a pony has many advantages for both buyer and seller. The most important is that negotiations to buy the pony can begin well in advance of the hand-over date, giving the buyer plenty of time to raise the money and to make arrangements for the pony's keep. In some cases the seller is willing to continue to keep the pony and to supervise his welfare, and the new rider, especially if inexperienced, can learn from the previous one.

If you are lucky enough to be offered a pony in this way, the chances are that he will suit you very well; otherwise, the offer would not have been made in the first place.

When you are just beginning to join the horsey community in your area, you may well see a pony that you think you might like for yourself. If you do not know the owners already, it is usually simple enough to find someone else who does and to discover whether the pony is likely to be offered for sale in the near future.

Even if the owners have not yet made up their minds, it is always worthwhile contacting them and asking for first refusal should they decide to sell at a later date. Provided that no one else is interested in him, you would stand an excellent chance of getting the pony. From the owners' point of view, such an arrangement would save them the cost of advertising as well as reassuring them that the pony would be going to a good home.

If you do not know anyone locally who is about to put their pony on the market, the best way of finding out is to contact the District Commissioner of your local Pony Club branch. District Commissioners get to know most of what goes on within the branch, are usually familiar with the ponies ridden by their members and are the best people to help you if you need advice.

One word of warning: local ponies quickly acquire a local reputation. Even if you manage to buy an exceptional pony, don't be disheartened if you do not immediately achieve the same results as the previous rider. The twelve-month familiarity rule is just as important as if the pony had come from a long way away. The difference is that you will be in the public eye, so to speak, whilst you and your pony develop your relationship.

DEALERS

Never reject the services of a good horse-dealer. Whatever you may have heard to the contrary, those whose business it is to buy and sell ponies are not all rogues and charlatans. Their livelihood is dependent on satisfied clients and their reputation can easily be damaged. It is in their interest as well as yours to find you a suitable pony.

When selecting a dealer, word-of-mouth recommendation is important. A good one will be well-known locally and may do more than just act as a broker between seller and buyer. Many dealers have their own yards and will school a pony carefully until they are satisfied that he is well-mannered, responsive and ready for passing on to his new rider.

The main disadvantage of going to a dealer is that the price of the pony may be higher than if he were being sold privately. The dealer has to make a profit and will also try to recoup the expense of keeping the pony until a buyer is found.

Some dealers do not buy ponies for resale but prefer to put clients in touch with vendors, leaving them to carry out their own negotiations. But the vendor will already have agreed to pay a commission to the dealer and the asking price will almost certainly take this into consideration.

The advantage of using a dealer is that he will do his best to find a pony that is right for you. He may even be prepared to take the pony back if, within an agreed period, the animal proves unsuitable. And he will go on looking until he finds one that you like and can afford.

HORSE SALES

Good children's ponies are often sold at auction and may turn out to be a bargain. But sale-rings are no place for the inexperienced, as you have little redress if things go wrong.

Some auctioneering firms offer an extended warranty on all the animals which come under their hammer. The most common warranty, however, lasts only 24 hours. In all cases, the warranty guarantees soundness in wind and limb but does not cover temperament or suitability.

There is usually very little opportunity to try the pony out satisfactorily, though you will be able to look him over and have him run out, enabling you to study his conformation and action. At some sales, you may be able to ride him in a schooling paddock.

The catalogue should give you brief details on the pony's history and you can make enquiries as to why he is being sold, but you will not have a great deal of time in which to find out much about him.

A sale-ring, therefore, is not recommended to first-time buyers.

When trying a pony for the first time, make certain that you take an expert with you. An experienced grown-up should be able to spot any problems which you might miss.

4

Considerations When Choosing a Pony

Wherever you have learned that a pony is for sale, it is vitally important to know what type you are looking for.

CHOOSING A BREED

The British Isles provide the best source of ponies in the world. Other countries have indigenous breeds too, but nowhere else is there such a wide variety as in Great Britain and Ireland.

Although the quality of the herds of ponies running wild in their native habitat is controlled through the efforts of their owners and the various breed societies, you do not have to visit these areas in order to find a good example of the breed.

Stud farms specialising in Britain's native ponies can be found all over the country and many of them have ponies for sale, already broken and ready for selling on. So if you have set your heart on a Dartmoor or a New Forest pony, for example, the appropriate breed society could put you in touch with a breeder in your vicinity.

Alternatively, a visit to a local agricultural show or major horse show where classes are held for mountain and moorland ponies will give you a chance of seeing some of the best examples of the various breeds. The show catalogue usually publishes the name of the breeder.

Registered ponies of all the breeds are highly regarded and

The advantage of a Shetland is its size. This very young rider can relate to a small pony and clearly feels confident and secure. A disadvantage is the breadth of the pony's back – the rider's legs barely reach to the bottom of the saddle flap. At this age, the child should never be left without supervision.

every breed has its devotees. Many children's ponies, however, are of uncertain breed, although they may show Welsh or New Forest characteristics. Almost all ponies will have enough native blood to make them hardy, sure-footed and good doers.

If you have no idea what sort of pony you are looking for, there are a number of points to remember when making your choice.

AGE

Do not buy a young pony. Any pony under the age of five will not be allowed to take part in Pony Club branch competitions and championships. Although you would be able to take a four-year-old to rallies, a pony of this age is still growing and will not have developed the muscles capable of negotiating a show-jumping or cross-country course. Temperamentally he may be quiet and obedient but, unless you are experienced, he could become difficult to manage as he grows older and stronger. Turning a young unschooled pony into a well-mannered, responsive ride can provide great satisfaction, but the process needs great patience, knowledge and understanding. (See *Training the Young Horse*, a Pony Club publication, for more information.)

The best ages are between eight and twelve years old. At eight, a pony is just entering his prime; at twelve, he has sufficient experience of life, especially if he has been well ridden and looked after, for even a novice rider to get tremendous pleasure from him.

A pony who has reached his teens can still be a good buy, although you should remember that when you have outgrown him and wish to sell him, the nearer he is to twenty the harder it will be to find a good home for him.

'First' ponies, the ones who take great care of beginners but are not expected to do anything at all strenuous, can be older than twenty. However, all old ponies are more expensive to keep, needing to have their teeth rasped more often and to be given extra food to maintain their health and condition.

Most people know that you can tell the approximate age of a horse by looking at his teeth, but complete accuracy is possible only up to eight years old. After that, it is more difficult to be accurate. If you suspect that a pony is much older than claimed, you should look for other signs, such as hollows above the eyes, a thickening of the neck muscles and prominent hip bones. However, ponies are not issued with birth certificates and the seller of a pony may not know his animal's life history.

HEIGHT

Deciding on the right size of pony can be fraught with difficulty, and mistakes are often made.

For a young child to benefit from a pony, the more he or she can do for that pony the better. This means catching, grooming and tacking up, as well as riding him. Obviously a small child with a large pony will not be able to reach up to put a bridle over the pony's head or to place a saddle on his back. Grooming presents similar difficulties. Nevertheless, the pony may temperamentally be perfect for beginners, truly unflappable, easy to catch, content to walk when other ponies are cantering or to keep up with the others if that is what the rider wants.

Very small ponies may be wilful, naughty and ready to take advantage of their riders' weaknesses at the first opportunity.

The only reason for buying a pony that is too big for his

This rider is clearly too large for her pony and places an unfair burden on the pony's back.

This child is too small for his mount. However quiet the horse or pony, do not be tempted to buy one to 'grow into'.

This pony and rider are well matched for size, but in a year or two she may well have outgrown him. In the meantime he looks a nice sort who could suit his rider well.

rider must be his reliability. You should never buy a pony to 'grow into'. The chances are that your inability to cope with him will put you off riding long before the two of you are perfectly matched.

Up to the age of about nine or ten, most children ride purely by balance. Their legs are not long enough to be effective aids and they are not capable of sitting deep enough in the saddle to make the pony do what they want him to. If anything, they tend to use their hands to maintain their position, treating the reins as a kind of grab-rail and relying on the pony's good nature to keep them safe.

Of course there are exceptions, but the average very young rider has too little knowledge and experience to appreciate and practise the finer points of horsemanship.

Differences in the physique and development of a child can make it difficult to lay down rules for matching size of pony with age of child. The following can be no more than a guideline:

Pony's height	*Rider's age*
Under 11hh	Under 10
11 to 12hh	8 to 11
12 to 13hh	9 to 14
13 to 14hh	10 to 15
14 to 14.2hh	13 to 16

A small, light fourteen-year-old can ride a 12.2hh pony very effectively, just as a tall ten-year-old can skilfully handle a pony of 14.2hh, particularly if he or she has several years' riding experience to draw on.

A child whose pony is too small is said to be 'under-mounted'; one with too big a pony is 'over-mounted'. If you expect your pony to last for three or four years and you have no younger brothers or sisters to take over when you move on, it is best to look at ponies within a height range of about 1½hh. In other words, if you are twelve years old and of average height and riding ability, you should look at ponies 13–14.2hh. If you are long and thin, with tall parents, a 14–

14.2hh pony will probably last you until you are sixteen. If you are small, with short legs, 13–13.2hh could serve you very well over the next four years.

Remember that the physique of a pony can make him look bigger or smaller than his measured height might suggest. A slightly built, fine-boned 12.2hh pony will look taller than a chunky 12.2hh with a low head carriage. A 14.2hh pony with substance, a short back and strong muscular quarters – especially if he carries his head high – will be well up to the weight of even a tall rider.

In general, the length of the rider's legs presents less of a problem than the length of the torso. Many young riders going through a fast-growing phase can start to look leggy on a pony yet still manage to achieve a high level of success. The reason is that their weight is still well within the pony's capabilities and the extra length of leg does not materially alter their centre of gravity. It is much more difficult for a pony to balance himself correctly if the rider's body – that is, the part above the saddle – is too long. Very often it is at this stage that a rider begins to realise that she has finally outgrown a beloved pony, usually because the pony can no longer carry her successfully round a cross-country course and is beginning to stop at jumps that he would once have flown over.

In fact, the odd refusal in a normally good, willing jumping pony is more likely to be due to the rider having grown taller **above the saddle** than to the pony having been over-jumped, over-faced or otherwise driven to boredom.

CONFORMATION

Many excellent children's ponies do not have perfect conformation, and those ponies which do come close to the ideal are likely to be so successful in competition that their selling price is high.

The average would-be buyer, therefore, operating on a limited budget, must be prepared to overlook some conformation faults. It is important to know which ones to ignore.

Three ponies of similar size but very different in type. All have their good points. ABOVE: Some Thoroughbred blood in this mare's ancestry accounts for her build, fine bone structure and length of back. The pony shown ABOVE RIGHT is typical of good native stock, with well-rounded quarters, a large eye and a deep girth. The skewbald (RIGHT) is a more cobby type and her head is coarser, but she has a neat compact build, good bone and a generous eye. Despite their differences, all three ponies could be good buys for the right child.

Whenever you are judging the conformation of a pony, it is important to take someone experienced with you. They may spot some vital fault that you have missed and it helps to be able to discuss the pony with someone who has seen him before making up your mind.

Head and neck A large, coarse head is often allied to a thick, heavily-muscled neck and crest. Unless the rider has a strong seat and legs, the pony will tend to lean on the bit, which in turn makes the rider heavy handed. Such a pony is

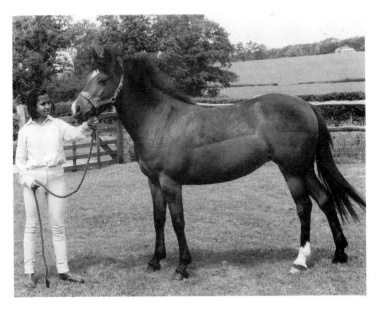

not a comfortable ride and will do little for the child who owns him.

Look for a neat head, big, kind eyes and trim, pricked ears. The head should be in proportion to the rest of the body, well set on a gently curving neck, and carried high but not so high that the nose sticks out.

The pony must have a snaffle mouth for in many competitions an ordinary jointed or straight-bar snaffle is the only permitted bit. A drop noseband or its equivalent, such as a grakle or flash, is acceptable since many ponies evade the bit by setting or crossing the jaw or opening their mouths.

Look at the angle at which the head joins the neck. The pony should be able to flex without restricting his breathing. Great depth from poll to jaw makes flexion difficult.

Chest A broad chest and deep girth indicate plenty of room for the lungs to expand, suggesting a pony with stamina. Avoid a pony which is particularly narrow in front, as the forelegs may be so close together that they interfere with each other, leading to brushing injuries (cuts on the inside of the leg when it is struck by the foot of the other leg).

Good breadth of chest is a characteristic of native ponies.

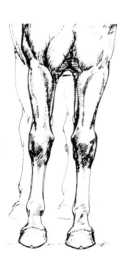

LEFT: Forelegs viewed from the front. Look for good width of chest; 'clean' limbs (straight and strong bones); knees that are large and flat, not puffy; and two front feet that are a pair.

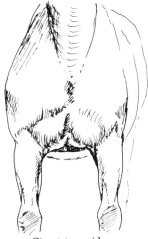

Chest too wide.

Chest weak and narrow – legs 'coming out of one hole'.

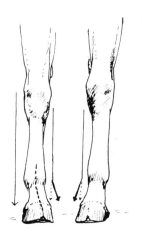

Pigeon toes (toes turning in).

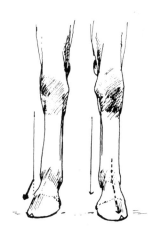

Toes turning out.

Shoulders   The slope of the shoulders is related to freedom of movement. In riding ponies, where a good, flowing action is required, a sloping shoulder is best. A more upright shoulder is indicative of pulling-strength and is often found in driving ponies. Ponies broken to harness are often advertised as 'ride and drive' but pulling a trap develops neck and shoulder muscles and shortens the stride, all of which make them a more uncomfortable ride.

If you have an interest in driving ponies, a ride-and-drive specialist will enable you to enjoy both aspects of pony-ownership and to continue with the pony when you have grown too big to ride him. Driving ponies are also likely to be very safe on the roads, even in heavy traffic. But you will find it difficult to improve your riding technique on one of them.

Withers   The withers are the highest point of the pony's back and the place where the pony is measured, his height being the distance from the top of the withers to the ground. Although in some parts of the world metric measurements are used for horses and ponies, the traditional 'hand' is still used in the English-speaking world. A hand is four inches (10 cm). Shetland ponies are usually measured in inches.

A pony aged six years or over may be issued with a Joint Measurement Board life certificate. This states that the pony has been accurately measured under specific conditions by an officially appointed measurer. A height certificate is useful if you intend to enter the pony in height-limited classes.

The shape of the withers does not affect the pony's action, but if they are unusually high or low, there may be difficulty in finding a saddle which fits the pony correctly. Many low-withered ponies need a crupper to prevent the saddle from slipping forward, whilst a high-withered animal could require a breast-plate to keep the saddle in place.

Back   The outline of the back should be slightly concave from the withers to the quarters. A deep hollow is a sign of weakness or old age, the back tending to get hollower as the pony grows older. Straight or roach backs (slightly convex) are both faults to be avoided as they indicate that the pony is incapable of carrying any weight and may lead to back problems.

A short back is usually strong but may restrict the pony's movements. A long back, unless it is well-muscled and linked to powerful quarters, may be weak as the extra length is usually between the saddle and the loins.

A prominent spine is not often seen on native ponies

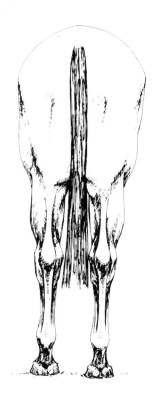

Quarters and hind legs viewed from behind. Look for strong, clean muscles; hocks that are clearly defined and powerful; and clean legs below the hock.

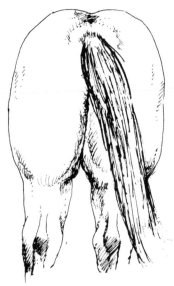

Heavy, overloaded quarters –
undesirable.

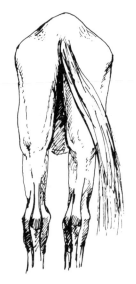

Weak, poor quarters; 'cut up
behind'.

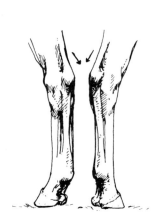

Cow hocks – a weakness.

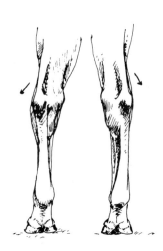

Hocks turned out – a
weakness.

unless they are undernourished; grass-fed ponies are far more likely to have pads of fat running on either side of the backbone. These can lead to difficulties in saddle fitting but do make them very comfortable for riding bareback.

Quarters The pony's hindquarters are the source of power and propulsion. Good quarters are rounded and well-muscled, with a gentle slope to the root of the tail. If the slope is pronounced (goose rump), the pony may not score points in a showing class but may well be a good jumper; it is not a serious fault unless you have showing ambitions.

Legs Even sturdy ponies have quite slender legs which look too frail to bear the weight of their tough little bodies. It is not surprising, therefore, that many people believe the legs to be the most important part of a horse, and they are certainly an area where most problems can arise.

When first inspecting a pony, make certain that he is standing on level ground. Then view him first from the side and then from front and rear:

- The pony should stand four-square and the forelegs should be straight from shoulder to pastern.
- The knees should be flat. Similarly, in the hind legs the area between stifle and hock (the second thigh) should be long and deep and the leg between the hock and fetlock straight.
- The hock itself should be broad when measured from front to back.
- The pasterns on all four legs should form a slope of roughly 45 degrees to the ground. Anything greater than this can put extra strain on the joints and tendons; though many ponies have quite upright pasterns without suffering any ill effects.
- When viewed from both front and rear, the legs should drop almost vertically to the ground. Any deviation is a potential weakness, perhaps leading to joint or tendon injury. There should be a good space between the two front legs at the top.

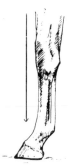

Good foreleg showing: large flat
knee; short cannon bone, clear of
puffiness or blemish; correct
pastern and hoof.

Good hind leg: correct angle;
hock clean and free from
puffiness or blemish.

Over at the knee – a weakness.

Sickle hock – a weakness.

Back at the knee –
a more serious weakness.

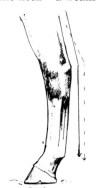

Straight hock – a weakness.

After looking at the pony standing still, examine him at the trot, both coming towards you and going away (see also page 59). His action should be straight and true, although many ponies have a tendency to twist their forefeet outwards as they move (dishing). If the foot flicks inwards, inspect the inside of the fetlock joint for any signs of an old injury.

Always remember that legs which are not quite perfect or movements that are not quite straight need not necessarily put you off buying the pony. In some cases, careful shoeing

Well-shaped hoof: round and open; frog large and healthy; strong hoof wall; sole slightly concave.

Boxy hoof: contracted heels; shrivelled frog; flat sole.

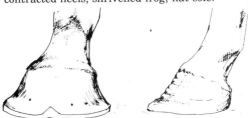

ABOVE LEFT: Large, flat foot – undesirable. ABOVE RIGHT: Foot showing laminitic rings and concave appearance; the toe is very long and the weight is back on the heels.

51

can minimise a problem, and for events where extra strain is put on the legs, such as jumping and cross-country, boots and bandages will help to protect the limbs.

Hooves Most native ponies have naturally hard hooves, with good horn. If the horn looks brittle and is cracking or breaking, ask the owners whether this is a chronic problem and what steps have been taken to cure it.

Hooves with heavily pronounced ridges are a sign of past illness, in small ponies often indicating a bout of laminitis. Examine the bottom of each foot. The frog should be well shaped and the sole slightly concave. A dropped sole and a misshapen frog are also legacies of laminitis.

A good sign of irregular, uneven action is the state of the shoes. If they show uneven wear, or more pronounced wear in one foot, some fault in conformation is sure to be the cause.

Hoof colour is usually unimportant. Some people believe that light-coloured hooves denote weak horn, but even experts disagree on this point.

Blemishes Old scars need not be a deterrent unless you are hoping to show the pony. Few ponies go through life without the occasional cut or tear and as long as they are not likely to interfere with the pony's action they can usually be ignored. Scars on the front of the knees (broken knees) are a sign that at sometime or other the pony has taken a fall on to his knees on hard ground and it is worth inquiring about the circumstances that caused such an injury. Might the pony be a natural stumbler?

TEMPERAMENT

This is possibly the most important feature of a pony and it is also the hardest to judge at a single inspection.

Just like humans, ponies can have nice natures, nasty natures, even a mixture of the two. They can be easy to handle or may need firm treatment. They can take a liking to one rider and be difficult with another. They can behave perfectly in a bridle or headcollar but be snappy and bad-tempered in the field or stable.

Generally speaking, the length of time that a pony has spent with his present owner is a good indication of his nature. People vary in the effort they are prepared to put in to overcome problems with a new pony, and some will abandon the struggle after a few weeks whilst others are still talking about 'teething troubles' after eighteen months. But any family which keeps a pony for two years or more is likely to have found his nature congenial, so a five- or six-year stay in one home is a recommendation in itself.

Always observe how the pony reacts when you – a stranger – approach him for the first time. If your first sight of him is in a stable, note whether his ears prick when you go towards him. He, of course, is in familiar surroundings; you are the intruder. The pony should be extremely curious to know what is going on. If he shows little or no reaction – if, for example, he goes on eating his hay or lays his ears back at the sight of you – he is either very hungry or very dull or, worse, bad-tempered and irritable.

Many ponies behave differently once they have a rider on their back. Some ponies gain great confidence from a rider. This shows itself when the pony meets something 'spooky' such as a noisy tractor or a big, fluttering paper bag. A led pony may mentally transform the tractor into a dragon and the paper bag into an evil ghost and may flatly refuse to go near either. A ridden pony may feel protected and comforted by his rider's presence, especially if the rider is calm and unflurried and talks to him in a soothing voice.

Some ponies are perfect gentlemen in the field or stable yard but become pig-headed and wilful when the rider is in the saddle. Others take any invitation to go faster than a collected trot as an exhortation to gallop. This, it must be admitted, is often due to the previous owner's behaviour when riding. Wild, careless riding almost invariably leads to wild, careless ponies and you should try to avoid galloping – or even cantering – at the same place every day.

Physical appearance can give clues to a pony's temperament. A big, kind eye suggests a kind nature; a small mean eye, with lots of white showing, indicates lack of generosity; an eye rolling back implies nervousness. A wall eye looks peculiar because the iris lacks pigment and the eye appears to be bluish-white around the pupil. However, it does not affect the pony's vision, and although wall-eyed ponies are said to be ill-tempered, this is not necessarily so; many good, generous ponies with wall eyes have served their owners faithfully and well.

GENDER

Whether you buy a mare or gelding is entirely a matter of personal preference. There may, however, be a practical reason for choosing one or the other if you have made arrangements to keep your pony in a field where others are kept. Generally speaking it is considered wiser to separate the sexes, as mares tend to behave 'marishly' or provocatively when there is a male around, and geldings may quarrel over a mare. This may sound strange, as geldings have been castrated to eliminate a stallion's characteristics (thick, crested neck, excitable temperament and sexual interest in females), but some vestigial awareness of mares does remain and geldings will often behave quite skittishly with them.

Before even going to look at a pony for sale, always consult the people with whom you plan to share the field as to whether they have any misgivings about mixing up the sexes. You may find the perfect little mare, but if the field is full of geldings you may have to make other arrangements for her keep or not buy her at all.

Those who love mares will readily describe their virtues – bolder, braver, more beautiful than geldings. Gelding fans will tell you how strong, kind and dependable they are. It is certainly true that mares can be temperamental, sometimes behaving in a silly manner for no apparent reason. Yet most top polo players prefer mares to geldings, mainly for their courage and intelligence, while top eventers seem to choose geldings (at Badminton in 1990, for example, there were only three mares among the 99 horses entered). In the end, the choice is yours.

Be careful, however, not to buy a 'rig'. This is the term applied to a gelding who has been imperfectly castrated or a horse in which one or both testes have not dropped. The latter may be sold as a gelding, but his instincts will be those of a stallion and he would not be safe for use as a child's pony.

A stallion, in fact, should never be bought for a child. Even a well-broken stallion, with an experienced rider, cannot be used for Pony Club activities unless the written permission of the District Commissioner is given.

COLOUR

Colour is not important in choosing a pony, although most people have their preferences.

There are many old wives' tales concerning colour and you can believe them if you like, but it would be foolish to turn down a pony who is perfect in every other respect simply because you are not happy with his colour.

What is certain about the colour of a pony is that the darker the colour, the easier it is to make him look smart. The summer coats of dark chestnuts, bays, browns and blacks can be made to shine like well-polished shoes with comparatively little effort, and, because the horn of the hooves of these ponies tends to be dark as well, the application of a little hoof-oil before the start of a showing class will send the pony into the ring looking spick and span.

The main disadvantage of a dark pony is that the coat readily shows dust, which in a field-kept pony is almost unavoidable.

Grey ponies, particularly those who are so light as to appear white, seem to flaunt grass and dirt stains and will need a great deal of effort to make them look their best. White markings on any horse need extra attention on showing days, although much can be achieved by applying powdered chalk.

5

Trying a Pony

Most sellers of ponies like to have them well groomed, tacked up and ready for the potential buyer to try. It is, after all, only natural to want to present the pony in a good light.

When you set off to look at a pony for sale, try to keep as open a mind as possible. In your excitement – and trying out a pony for the first time is indeed an exciting experience –

First introduction to a pony which looks ideally suited to a young rider who is past the 'baby' stage but still young enough to need a quiet, tractable pony that she can handle with confidence.

The prospective owner is happy to take the lead rope herself. The next stage will be to see how she manages in the saddle.

you may have already endowed the pony with perfect qualities. But it is essential to resist any tendency to overlook faults; if you have any misgivings at all, you must voice them. Even if you have already drawn cash from the building society or your parents are ready with the chequebook, TAKE YOUR TIME. Buying a pony is a big step, and you must be as sure as possible that you are not making a mistake.

Wear suitable riding clothes. If you turn up in old jeans and admit that you have forgotten your crash hat, the present owners of the pony may be able to lend you a hat but they will not be very impressed with your efficiency. They may even decide that they will not sell their precious pony to you after all. Anyone who forgets a hat could easily forget to check the pony's water. So try to make a good impression.

The pony will probably be waiting in the stable, groomed, tacked up and ready to go. If you arrive, say, a quarter of an hour early, you may be in time to see the pony being saddled and bridled, and this can be helpful.

57

Once you have arrived, the owner/rider will probably put the pony through his paces, normally in a paddock or school, depending on what facilities are available. The pony will doubtless be jumped over two or three small jumps.

While this is going on, you should observe the pony closely. Note how much effort the rider has to exert and how quickly the pony responds. If he is put into a canter or gallop, see how quickly he comes back to hand. Remember that he is going over familiar jumps, and note whether his performance seems listless or whether he goes forward eagerly, with his ears pricked.

Watch his movements. Are his paces smooth and flowing? Is he difficult to stop? Is he obedient? Does the rider carry a whip; if so, how often is it used?

When it is your turn to try the pony, demonstrate that you know what you are doing. Before gathering your reins and getting on (from the correct side), talk to the pony and stroke his nose. Make certain that you are comfortable in the saddle, and adjust your stirrups before moving off. Walk the pony while you are getting accustomed to his stride and, when you want to increase the pace, remember the instruction you received at your riding school.

If the jumps seem too high for you, do not be too shy to ask for them to be lowered. You know that the pony will jump the prescribed height, but there is no loss of face in admitting that you would rather start small on a strange pony.

After your ride, bring the pony back, stand for a moment, and then dismount. All the time, you should be observing how he behaves. Never forget to talk to him.

Now is the time to examine him from the ground. First of all, remove the saddle and run your hands over his head, neck and body, noting his reactions. Run your hand down each leg in turn and see how readily he allows each foot to be picked up. Feel for bumps and scars.

If you have taken the sensible precaution of bringing an experienced adviser with you, he or she will probably carry out an examination as well, which should include inspecting the pony's teeth.

The pony should then be run up in hand. This is a good test of how well the pony leads, and should be carried out on level, hard ground or concrete, trotting to you and away from you and circling clockwise and anti-clockwise, while your adviser observes from the front and behind. Any faults in the pony's action should be apparent.

Watch particularly for signs of lameness, which can be extremely difficult to detect. Generally speaking, if the lameness is in a front leg, the pony's head will nod forwards as the sound leg comes to the ground, raising the head again when the lame leg comes to the ground.

When the pony is trotted up in hand, watch for faults in his action.

With hind-leg problems, the pony leans towards the sound side and may lift his quarters slightly or drag a toe on the painful side.

Severe lameness shows at the walk, but trot is needed to expose slight lameness, and even then it may be hard to decide whether the problem is in the front or rear legs.

At this stage most sellers will be tactful enough to give the prospective buyers a chance to have a discussion among themselves. Remember that on your first visit you will not be viewing all aspects of the pony. You will not, for example, be able to tell if he is easy to catch, so you must remember to ask if the owners ever have problems in getting him in from the field.

In fact, before coming to any decision there are a great many questions which you should ask the present owners and you should bring a list with you.

Only the most unscrupulous owner will tell you a downright lie, but it is very easy for perfectly honest vendors to forget to provide relevant information or to overlook some aspect of the pony which is important to you. Here are a few guidelines to questions you should ask, together with the answers you may receive:

Is the pony easy to (1) catch, (2) shoe, (3) box, (4) clip? The answer to all four should be yes. If the seller hesitates, try to pin her down. Perhaps the pony has never been clipped. Perhaps he reacts badly to hot shoeing but is quiet when being shod cold. Maybe he can be caught 99 per cent of the time but occasionally has an off day. It is up to you to decide how much of a drawback an unfavourable answer might be.

Has the present owner used a box, or a trailer? Does the pony load easily going, and returning? A pony may happily load in a box but refuse to go into a trailer, or vice versa. A poor loader must give you pause for thought. Even if at the moment you do not intend to box to shows (you may have no trailer), there is nothing more frustrating than a pony who gives trouble when asked to load. Reluctant loaders can be cured, usually by feeding them in the trailer or box until they come to connect the vehicle with a pleasant experience. But this takes time and patience. The ideal pony is one who walks up the ramp as soon as it is lowered, stands quietly while others are loaded or the breeching straps are fastened, and then remains quiet when the ramp is lowered on arrival. Fortunately, there are plenty of these ponies about.

Will he (1) live alone, (2) be left alone, (3) leave other ponies, (4) behave well alone?

The answer to all four should be yes. If not, be cautious. Most ponies when left alone in a field will make a lot of noise, run up and down the fence line a few times and then resign themselves to waiting for their companions to return. This can be annoying but is not too serious. Others may try to

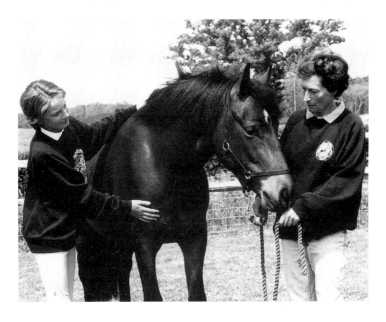

Always handle the pony before riding him. It is a point in his favour if he allows you to run your hand over his body without backing away, flinching or putting his ears back.

61

jump the fence, which could lead to injury or to a loose pony on the roads: both very worrying situations. A nappy pony, who is reluctant to go away from others, will cause a great deal of stress to an inexperienced rider.

Does he kick/bite other ponies?

The answer you should hope for is *never*. A pony who kicks in company is more trouble than he is worth. Tying a red ribbon to his tail would not absolve you from responsibility if he kicked out and injured another pony.

Does he kick/bite people?

The answer here must be *never*. Bad-tempered ponies should be left to experienced handlers. For the first-time pony-owner, confidence in the pony's good temper is paramount.

Will he lead, both in hand and from another pony?

If the answer is no, or reluctantly, you must decide, in the light of what you intend to do with him, whether this is important or not. In mounted games a good leader is essential.

Does he mind being saddled and bridled?

This depends on how strong-willed you are. A pony who throws up his head when you try to pass the head-piece of the bridle over his ears will require a great deal of patience on your part to cure him of the habit. Saddling up is not usually a problem, though some ponies have 'cold backs', which means that they tend to hump their backs when the saddle is first put in place and to buck or otherwise misbehave when the rider first gets on. In the latter case, a good, thick numnah and a time lapse between putting on the saddle and mounting may offer a solution.

Pulling faces, laying back ears and nipping are not uncommon reactions when the girths are fastened. The usual reason is ticklishness or undue sensitivity and you are unlikely to cure the pony of this habit, but it is quite possible to keep out of harm's way when fastening the girths.

If possible, try a prospective pony on the road. Here, in a country lane, a grass verge can help to keep the pony away from traffic. Always be alert when on the road, not only for passing cars but also for unexpected hazards in the hedge or verge.

Is he head-shy?

Many ponies are sensitive around the poll and dislike having their ears touched or their mane pulled in this region. This can make mane-plaiting, for example, very difficult. Think twice before buying a head-shy pony. In severe cases, the pony may flinch as soon as a hand is raised towards his head. This suggests that at some time in the past he has been hit around the head. Again, you should be cautious about buying such a pony. Memories of bad experiences are extremely difficult to eradicate.

How does he react to dogs, traffic (including tractors and motorbikes) and men?

Adverse answers to any of these questions should raise doubts in your mind. Dogs seem to be an integral part of the horsey world, and though you may not be a dog-owner yourself, your friends may have one. It takes a very strong friendship to survive the kicking of a dog by a pony. Cars, tractors and motorbikes are hard to avoid: if a pony's owners have not managed to cure him of being frightened of them, it is unlikely that *you* will be successful.

A pony who has been roughly handled in his youth by a man can develop a lifelong aversion to men and it requires a very patient, gentle and quiet man to overcome such fear. Even if the men in your household never have anything to do with the pony, you may well have a male blacksmith and a male vet, both of whom are essential to your pony's well-being. Question the seller very carefully on this point to discover the extent of the pony's mistrust.

Does he live out in winter?
Most native breeds take happily to wintering out, as they develop thick coats which are ample protection against the weather. Your arrangements for the upkeep of your new pony are therefore likely to include living out the whole year round. Find out about the routine that the previous owner has been following, and remember that a hardy native pony is better off without a New Zealand rug unless he has been extensively clipped. An owner with stabling may have been in the habit of bringing the pony in at night, but in almost all cases this is for the owner's convenience rather than the pony's.

Does he crib-bite, wind-suck, weave, kick his stable down, paw the ground?
These are all stable vices, which can develop over a period of time in a stabled horse. The first three are usually due to boredom. Native ponies should not suffer from them – mainly because they are not likely to be left in a stable for long periods. Crib-biting, wind-sucking and weaving, however, can be learned from other horses and on rare occasions can be picked up by a pony in a field. Over a long period, they can have a debilitating effect on the pony's wind.

A pony who kicks the stable walls or paws the ground is trying to tell you how much he hates being stabled, and his actions can cause damage. Pawing the ground will wear out the toes of his shoes.

In what level of competitions has he taken part?

This is a good indication of the pony's ability. If he has qualified for a major competition, this will usually be reflected in his price.

Has he ever suffered from sweet-itch/laminitis?

Sweet-itch is a skin condition believed to be caused by an allergy to certain midges. Signs of sweet-itch are a ragged mane and tail, scabs and rawness. The midges are active in summer and cause intense irritation along the crest, around the head and in the tail and dock area. In order to find relief, the pony will rub the area against any available object, such as a tree or fence, often creating raw patches which may become infected. He may be restless, walking endlessly round and round the field.

Various treatment has been tried, ranging from expensive injections to patent lotions and fly-repellents, but the condition is incurable. A certain amount of control is possible with the fitting of a head and neck cover or by keeping the pony in at the times when the midges are at their worst – early morning and at dusk. However, unless you have the necessary facilities for this, you would be wise to reject any pony which suffers from this condition. [*Note*: During the winter, the pony's mane and tail grow thick again and if you are viewing the pony in the winter months, it is not possible to recognise a sweet-itch sufferer.

Laminitis is another affliction common to native ponies. It is a severe fever of the foot, usually caused by too much or too rich food and insufficient exercise. Spring is a particularly dangerous time for small ponies, who tend to gorge themselves on new grass. Once a pony has developed laminitis he is very susceptible to bouts of the disease. The usual signs that a pony has had laminitis in the past are heavy ridges on the hoof and, if the attack was severe, a dropped sole.

Has he ever been to Pony Club camp?
This is usually a good recommendation since it suggests: firstly, that the present owners are Pony Club people and will have cared for and ridden him in the approved way; and, secondly, that he is capable of taking part in company in Pony Club activities.

How long have you had him?
If the answer to this is anything over two years, it suggests that the pony has suited his present owners very well. If, however, the reply is a shorter time, there is no need to be discouraged. Ponies are sometimes bought to give a child confidence for one season only and the rider is now ready to go on to a pony with more scope. Children also have the annoying habit of growing several inches in a short time. The child may simply have grown too big for the pony more quickly than the parents expected.

Why are you selling him?
The answer to this is tied up with the answer to the previous question. An older pony, bought to give a child confidence, may have done his job efficiently and is now ready to pass on his expertise to another child. The pony may have taught all the children in the family and there are now no little ones left to take over. The family may be moving away or abroad. Or the child could have lost interest in riding or be about to study for exams. The present rider could now be ready for competitions which are beyond the present pony's ability. The reason for the sale should emerge in general discussion.

Once you are satisfied that the pony appears to suit you in all major aspects, you are ready to make an offer. Usually, an offer is made verbally, subject to vetting, and at this point, if the offer is accepted, a legal contract has been entered into, which can be enforced provided that the pony passes the vet's inspection.

In most cases the asking price is not open to negotiation and it is up to you to decide whether the amount is fair. Sometimes the price includes the pony's tack and other bits and pieces, such as headcollar and rugs, or the vendors may agree to sell them to you for an extra amount, depending on the value of the equipment.

It can be very useful to buy the pony's own saddle and bridle, as long as they are in good condition. Buying a well-fitting saddle for a pony is not just a matter of selecting one at your local saddlers because it is at a price that you can afford. It needs an expert to fit a saddle on a pony and the saddle must also be comfortable for the rider.

If you are buying a new bit or stirrup irons, it is better and safer to spend more on stainless steel, which will last a long time, than to save money by choosing an inferior metal, which can bend or break. A recent development in bit manufacture is the use of nylon for the mouthpiece. It is hard-wearing and very effective for some ponies.

With a private sale, do not expect to be allowed to have the pony on trial. Even if the sellers agree, a month or less is not really long enough for you reasonably to assess the pony's suitability. Anything longer than a week is not fair to the vendors. Dealers, however, may be more amenable to trial periods.

You should be prepared for private sellers to want to visit your home in order to see where the pony will be kept. This is not an intrusion into your privacy but a sensible precaution. An answer to an advertisement gives few clues to the nature of the enquirer, and most people are anxious for their much-loved pony to go to a good home. No one wants their pony to end up in an abattoir, and unscrupulous meat-men have been known to pose as genuine buyers, even going so far as to take a child along with them to try out the pony.

6

Having a Pony Vetted

It has now become the usual practice to have a pony checked over by the vet before you finally decide to buy him. This is expected by the vendor, who will not be offended by your request to have the pony vetted.

If you are seriously interested in a pony, it is wise to check that he has no hidden defects which could cause you expense and distress in the future. Normally, you contact a vet (not the one habitually used by the seller) and ask him to look the pony over.

You should tell the vet exactly what you hope to do with the pony once you have bought him. If you plan to hunt him through the season, or to use him for mounted games, general Pony Club activities or simply hacking around, let the vet know.

The vet will inspect the pony's teeth (assessing his age and checking whether the teeth need rasping), examine the legs and feet and listen to the pony's heart and lungs. He will point out any minor blemishes, such as scars or windgalls, and check for evidence of past illness, such as laminitis. He may carry out an analysis of the pony's dung to see whether there is any heavy parasitic infestation. And he will check the pony's movement and action for any hint of unsoundness.

Such an examination is not cheap. But once the pony has been passed sound you can be sure that he will be fit to carry out whatever work programme you plan for him, and the vet's fees can be regarded as money well spent. And it is worth taking the advice you have paid for.

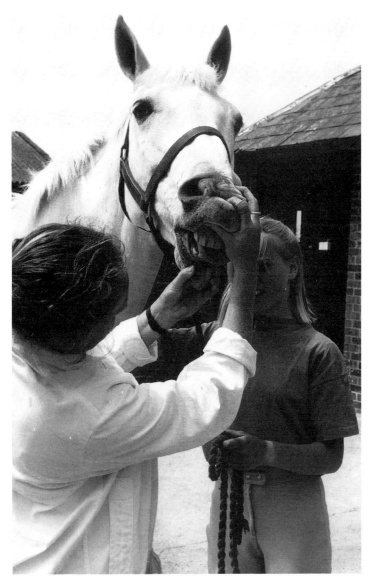

The vet will examine the pony's teeth to determine his age and to check whether they need rasping.

If, however, the pony fails the examination, you have to decide how important the defect is likely to be. The sellers may be genuinely amazed at the failure and will tell you quite truthfully that they have never had any problems. Indeed, it may be worthwhile to get a second opinion. No vet is infallible and the second examination may produce quite a different result. This, of course, leaves you with a dilemma. Which opinion – and remember that it is only an opinion – do you take?

If the pony is expensive, it may be worthwhile to have X-rays taken of the front feet and joints, but these add further to the cost. If you are not careful, the cost of carrying out a thorough examination may total more than the purchase price.

There is, of course, no obligation on your part to have the pony vetted at all. Many successful sales have been con-

Close examination of the backbone. Many problems, seemingly unrelated, may have their origin in disorders of the spine.

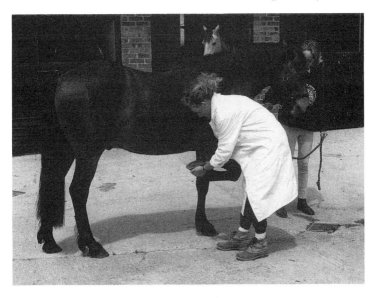

Inspecting a forefoot for signs of past disease or malformation.

cluded without a vet going anywhere near the animal, but this does depend on a high degree of mutual trust.

Should you decide to consult a vet, do make certain that he or she is an expert on the treatment of horses. If you have to look through the *Yellow Pages*, always check that the vet who will be examining the pony has an extensive equine practice.

7

A Pony on Loan

Lending a pony is common practice nowadays. It is the ideal solution for an owner who no longer needs the pony but who wishes to have some say in his future – provided, of course, that money is not an issue.

Usually, the potential borrower is contacted by the owner and offered the loan. For many children whose parents cannot afford the capital outlay it is their only chance of having a pony they can call their own. Loans may be arranged through an advertisement and sometimes the advertiser may offer a choice: 'for loan or sale' or 'for loan with a view to sale'.

It is unwise to take on a borrowed pony unless he fulfils the same criteria as if you were buying him. A borrowed pony needs the same care and attention as one you owned outright, and once you have him, a good lender will not interfere.

For the sake of both parties, it is wise to draw up a loan agreement. This states the conditions of the loan and describes the items which will accompany the pony and which should be returned with the pony when the period of the loan comes to an end.

It is not necessary to have the agreement notarised but both parties should sign and date the agreement and each keep a copy. A typical agreement could read as follows:

LOAN AGREED BETWEEN (name of lender) of (lender's address) and (name of borrower) of (borrower's address)

Name of pony .~~Rosie~~...........

Description of pony. ~~Grey~~

Height ~~14.1hh~~.................

Sex .~~Female~~................

Age .~~11 years~~.............

Items on loan with the pony .~~Saddle bridle~~........,........

....

....

1. (Borrower's name) agrees to keep the pony at (borrower's address) and undertakes not to move the pony or to lend him to a third party without the lender's permission.

2. The period of the loan shall be for a minimum of one year and may be terminated thereafter by either party with three months' notice on either side.

3. During the period of the loan, the borrower undertakes to maintain the pony at the borrower's expense, to meet all veterinary and shoeing bills, and to keep the pony's vaccinations and worming programmes up to date.

4. The borrower agrees to insure the pony for a sum acceptable to both parties.

5. Should the pony fall ill or be injured so severely that the vet recommends humane destruction, the lender should be consulted within an hour of the recommendation. If, however, the lender cannot be contacted and the delay would cause the pony unnecessary suffering, the borrower may take the decision without consultation.

Signed (date) ..~~January 1993~~............

Signatures of both borrower and lender. ....

A minimum limit for the period of loan is essential to make the borrowers appreciate that they are entering into a serious commitment. It would be most unfair to the lender to have the pony returned within a few days or a month. If circumstances arise within the first year which make it impossible for the borrower to keep the pony, the clause can be waived on agreement from both sides.

The paragraph about having the pony destroyed sounds macabre, but it is important. Accidents can happen all too quickly, especially on the roads, and a pony is a vulnerable creature. A severely injured pony should not be left to suffer simply because his legal owner happens to be out of the country or is away for the day, and anyone who lends her pony to someone else must presumably feel that that person can be trusted to make the right decision.

Lending is an excellent method of ensuring that an outgrown and much-loved pony continues to lead a useful, fulfilled life. When the period of loan comes to an end, another borrower can usually be found and when the pony finally grows too old to work, you could be in a position to give him a happy retirement.

It is important not to push an active pony into premature retirement, even if you have the facilities to keep him. Most ponies thrive on work and enjoy the variety that comes from being ridden, going to rallies and taking part in shows. It is fairer to him to give some other child the opportunity to enjoy him as much as you have done.

There is one other point to make about the advantages of lending. Selling a pony is traumatic, particularly if the pony has served you well. Even the acquisition of a new pony cannot completely banish the pain of parting, and it is very hard to come to terms with the fact that you may never see the pony again and never know what happens to him in the future. But a pony on loan is not going out of your life for ever. Although the borrower may later ask to buy him, you and your new pony will by then have built up a partnership and it will be easier to come to a decision.

'For loan with view to sale' is a good way of easing the distress of saying goodbye to a pony.

8

Tack and Equipment

First-time owners find buying tack and equipment one of the most difficult aspects of acquiring a pony. If you have been unable to buy the pony's tack from the previous owner, you will obviously have to start from scratch. A good saddler should be able to help you, but if you are unlucky enough to be served by an indifferent or uninterested assistant you may have to make many trips to the tack shop before you are satisfied.

The following information may help you:

Headcollar   These are available in nylon or leather. Nylon is cheap and widely used. It comes in a variety of colours and is generally hard-wearing. Leather headcollars must be treated with saddle-soap or other proprietary leather preservative to keep them supple. Headcollars have metal fittings (rings, buckles, etc); brass is the most durable but adds to the cost. Fastenings may be tongued buckles or looped buckles. The latter are cheaper but can slip. Headcollars are usually available in four sizes: foal, pony, cob and full.

Halter   A very cheap alternative to the headcollar is a halter, which consists of a simple hemp strap which passes over the poll and round the nose, finishing with an integral rope which knots under the chin. It is useful as a spare but is not a substitute for a headcollar.

Lead-rope   Made of plaited cotton, nylon or jute, the lead-rope usually fastens to the headcollar by means of a spring

Headcollar – leather or nylon webbing.

Webbing halter.

clip. Some jute lead-ropes have a loop at one end. The free end is passed through the ring at the back of the headcollar then through the loop, and the rope is pulled tight. The rope cannot come undone but nor can it be easily removed, especially if it is wet. A spring clip is best.

Bridle Bridles are sold in three sizes: pony, cob and full. The price quoted will not include the bit, but it should cover browband and cavesson noseband. The reins may or may not be included. Portions of a bridle are also sold separately. If, for example, your pony needs a drop noseband instead of a cavesson, the saddler may be willing to make up the bridle, substituting the drop for the cavesson, but not all saddlers are willing to do so. Hardwearing bridles made of nylon are widely available and are useful as spare bridles. They can be laundered in a washing machine.

When selecting reins, choose a pair that are a suitable length for your pony and the right thickness to feel comfort-

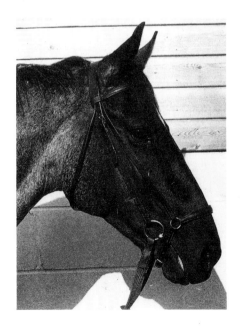

Correctly fitted snaffle bridle with a drop noseband.

An ordinary snaffle bridle with a cavesson noseband, fitted with a loose-ringed jointed snaffle bit.

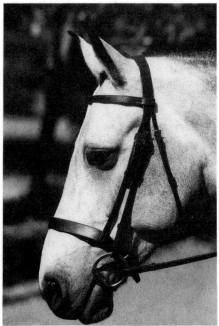

Correctly fitted snaffle bridle with a cavesson noseband.

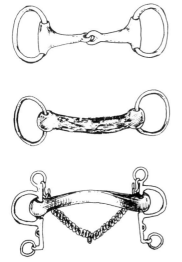

Commonly used bits – TOP: eggbutt snaffle; CENTRE: plain rubber snaffle – a mild bit; BOTTOM: Vulcanite or rubber pelham with double-linked curb chain (may be suitable for a strong pony). When choosing a bit make sure that the pony is comfortable and that the child is safe.

able in your hands. Plaited, Continental or rubber-covered reins improve grip.

Bit There are many different bits on the market, but a first pony should go well in a snaffle. This consists of a metal, rubber or nylon mouthpiece, with a ring at each end. The mouthpiece may have a joint in the middle. The rings may be loose (they move freely through the holes at the ends of the mouthpiece) or eggbutt (the mouthpiece broadens into a hinge where it joins the rings and whilst the rings pass through the hinge they cannot move round). The latter are popular for ponies as they cannot pinch the corners of the mouth.

A bit is measured in inches across the width of the mouthpiece, i.e. between the rings, in sizes rising in ½-in. units from 4½in. to 6 in. If the bit is a good fit, you should be able to put your index fingers snugly between the pony's mouth and the bit rings, when the bit is in the right position in the pony's mouth.

Stainless steel is the best metal for bits as it is strong and durable. Plated metal is cheaper and, although strong, can

A vulcanite or rubber pelham fitted with pelham roundings may be suitable if the pony is a little too strong for its rider.

chip and flake. Solid nickel is soft and can break and is not recommended. Rubber or vulcanite mouthpieces usually have a steel core. If you can afford it, opt for stainless steel.

Saddle   Most saddlers sell secondhand saddles, which are usually a good buy. The most important part of the saddle is the tree (internal framework), which must not be cracked or broken. It can be difficult to tell whether a tree has been damaged but as long as you have gone to a reputable saddler, you should be quite safe in buying a secondhand saddle.

Saddles are measured in inches and come in various shapes. Initially, choose a general-purpose saddle, preferably Pony Club approved. If the words 'Pony Club Approved' are stamped on the stirrup bar, the saddle will have been made to a master pattern kept at Pony Club headquarters. If the tree pattern has been submitted to the Pony Club and approved, the words will be stamped on the flap just above the bar.

Saddles are sold without girths, stirrup irons or stirrup leathers. The rider should feel comfortable in the saddle (try it out by sitting on it in the shop), but it must also fit the pony. If possible, take the pony to the saddlers to have the saddle fitted. If not, ask an expert to help you when you try the saddle on the pony. Most saddlers will allow you to take the saddle on approval or will visit your pony to advise on fitting the saddle.

Always inspect the girth straps for signs of cracking or wear. If necessary, any offending strap should be replaced. Three straps are better than two. At the same time, check that the safety catch on the stirrup bar has not rusted into the closed position nor become very loose.

A recent addition to the market, and widely advertised, are the saddles manufactured from man-made materials. These come in various colours, usually navy or black. They

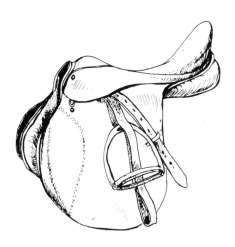

General-purpose saddle.

are fairly inexpensive and will not deteriorate if they get wet but some people do not find them comfortable. Bright colours, such as red or blue are not accepted by the Pony Club. Leather saddles are used in the show ring.

Buckle guards These are inexpensive D-shaped flaps of leather which thread on to the girth straps and protect the saddle flap from being worn by the girth buckles. They help to prolong the life of a saddle.

Girths Girths are available in a variety of materials: leather (durable but must be kept soft and supple to avoid girth galls); string (fairly inexpensive and strong, but can pinch); and, most popular, a cotton or nylon padded material, which is long-lasting and easy to wash. Webbing girths with single buckles were once popular, and were usually worn in pairs. They are no longer generally available, although you may find them offered in secondhand sales. Whilst cheap, they are not a good buy as they can become very stiff and may chafe or break.

Girths start at around 34in. and rise in 2-in. steps. A well-built 11.2hh Welsh pony would probably need a 38-in. girth. Before visiting the saddler, take the pony's girth measurement by passing a tape measure right round his body just behind the withers.

Leathers Do not buy leathers that are too long 'to allow for growth'. If the leather is too thick, the rider may find it uncomfortably bulky under the saddle skirt. The holes in some leathers are numbered, which is useful for remembering which length you normally use, but unless the leathers have been swapped over from time to time, an unbalanced rider may cause one of the leathers to stretch.

Irons For safety's sake, buy stainless steel. Accidents can happen if an inferior metal such as nickel bends or breaks. Wear jodhpur or riding boots when trying a stirrup iron for size. The correct size is one that is about ¾in. (2cm) wider

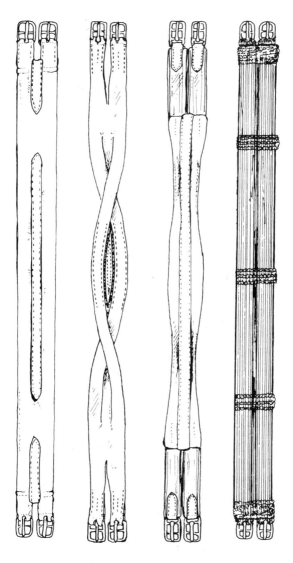

Suitable girths – FROM LEFT TO RIGHT: Cotton fabric with soft padded inner layer; leather Balding girth; leather Atherstone girth, shown with elastic panels at each end; string girth (cotton or nylon).

than the widest part of the boot. Safety stirrups have a removable rubber ring instead of the outer side of the iron. Replacement rings are cheap and easy to buy.

Grooming kit To start with, you will need: Hoof pick, Dandy brush, Body brush, Rubber or plastic curry comb, Sponges (for cleaning round eyes, nostrils and dock). All other items can be bought later. A cardboard box can be used to store the grooming kit, although a plastic box with lid, carrying handle and inside tray is preferable.

Tack-cleaning kit You will need: Saddle soap (available in tins or bars). Small sponges. Soft cloth for polishing metal work. Small bowl or bucket.

Buckets Plastic buckets are inexpensive. Mark the buckets with your name or your pony's.

Feed bowl(s) Choose a broad-bottomed bin which cannot be knocked over. Flexible rubber feed bowls with carrying handles are useful as they have no awkward corners where stale food can get trapped. In any case, food bowls should always be cleaned out after use.

All the items described above are necessary to start with. You will find that, later on, there are many other items to buy, such as leg guards, rugs, bandages and boots, but many of them can go on Christmas and birthday present lists.

SIZE CHART FOR TACK				
Size of pony	*Headcollar*	*Bridle*	*Bit*	*Saddle*
Under 11hh	Foal/ pony	Pony	4in.	14–15in.
11–12.2hh	Pony	Pony	4½in.	15–16in.
12.3–14hh	Pony/ cob	Pony/ cob	4½ – 5½in.	16in.
Over 14hh	Cob	Cob	5½in.	16–17in.

When buying anything made of leather, check that the item is British or Continental. Some Asian saddlery appears to be a bargain and looks good but the workmanship, particularly in those parts you cannot see, is often crude and the leather itself may have been improperly prepared. The result is a vital piece of equipment which could break when under stress or stretch when wet; in either case, this could lead to serious injury to both pony and rider.

If you need advice about any item that you intend to buy, always go to an expert. Your local Pony Club branch will certainly give you help.

9

Bringing Your Pony Home

The vet has passed the pony; the price has been agreed; the cheque has been cleared; the days of waiting are over, and your pony is coming home.

This is the most exciting day of your life; and for the sake of your pony and yourself you should try to plan it carefully.

Whether you have borrowed a trailer to collect the pony, or someone is bringing him for you, or you have decided to hack him home because he is not very far away, try to arrange for him to arrive in the morning.

In most cases, the pony will be living in a field with others. The ponies will have already sorted out their pecking order, and they are unlikely to treat a stranger like a long-lost friend.

When two ponies meet for the first time, their initial reactions are to sniff noses, stamp and squeal. Then, depending on the newcomer's behaviour – submissive and deferential or bossy and aggressive – the old hands will either leave him alone or turn their quarters on him and show him their heels. The boss of the field may go further, nipping and biting the newcomer, chasing him around or lashing out whenever he comes within range.

Your pony should be able to take care of himself but you must give him every chance to keep clear of trouble. This means turning him out **in daylight** – so that he can see a kick coming – and not putting him into a small, heavily-populated field where he could find himself trapped in a corner.

If his arrival is during the late afternoon or early evening, try to keep him overnight in a stable or in a small paddock on his own, turning him out with the others in the morning when the whole day lies ahead.

Sometimes it is necessary to make the introduction a gradual one, in which case you will need to have some knowledge of the other ponies or horses in the field. A bossy horse or pony who has formed an attachment to one of his companions and merely tolerates the rest can be dangerously aggressive towards a newcomer. This situation is fortunately rare, but if it does exist, the only solution is to put your new pony in an adjoining field for, say, a week, preferably on his own. He can then make the acquaintance of all the horses, including the aggressive one, while remaining safely on his side of the fence.

Eventually, however, the pony must join the others. Try to avoid feeding time, when rivalry is likely to be at its height. Wait until the other ponies are well away from the gate, then open the gate and lead your pony through, turning him to face the gate before removing his lead-rope. Until you are certain that your pony is easy to catch, it is wise to leave him in a well-fitted headcollar. After a week or two, you should be able to turn him out without one.

Wait for a while to note what happens. Usually the new pony stands for a moment, taking stock. When he sees the others, he may whinny and will then set off towards them, head up, ears pricked. They, in their turn, will move towards him.

Do not be alarmed at the squealing and stamping which will almost certainly follow their meeting. It only lasts a few minutes. Eventually, the other ponies will begin to lose interest. As they return to their grazing, your pony, too, will begin to graze. At first, he will graze alone; indeed, it may be a week or more before he is allowed to graze within touching distance of the others but as the relationship between them develops, the pony will become part of the herd.

He may make friends with just one of the others. When you visit him, you will find him nose to nose with his new companion. By then, his position in the social order will be established.

There is no way of telling in advance whether your pony is a leader or a follower unless his previous owners mention the fact. The gentlest pony to handle can turn out to be a real bully in the herd, while the bossiest and most bad-tempered pony in the stable can be a coward in the field.

Do not worry about showing your pony the whereabouts of the water-trough. He is quite capable of finding that out for himself.

On your pony's first day, turn him into the field, watch him for a while and then go home and leave him to settle down. You can return later to see how he is getting on, but for his first day he should be left in peace.

It is very tempting to catch him, ride him, and show him off to all your friends, but it will be better for the pony to let him adjust to his new surroundings quietly and without fuss. It will not be long before he gets to know you and recognises your voice, but you must give him at least twenty-four hours to settle in.

10

Insurance and Legal Responsibilities

A pony becomes your legal responsibility when his purchase price has been handed over to the vendors (allowing time for the cheque to be cleared) and the pony has been moved to his new home.

At this stage it is extremely important for you to be insured for personal liability. Many householders' policies include a personal liability clause, which would cover you in the event of your pony causing damage or injury to someone else and a claim being made against you. You will also be covered against third-party claims if you are a fully paid-up member of the Pony Club, whose insurance policy offers personal liability protection to all members.

However, most owners feel that it is sensible to insure their animals against happenings in which personal liability does not arise.

Insurance can be arranged through an insurance broker or directly through an insurance company. Equestrian magazines often carry advertisements for horse insurance which merely entail filling in the proposal form included with the ad and sending the appropriate fee.

All insurance proposals cover death or theft of the horse and personal liability of the owner. Most have other forms of cover which are optional and usually attract a higher premium.

In most cases, basic cover would include death by accident,

illness or injury, theft, personal liability and limited and varied funds for permanent injury to the rider. Situations in which these could occur are listed and extra premiums are charged if the list includes activities which the company would regard as particularly risky – such as hunting, cross-country riding and hiring the pony out.

As well as the basic cover, owners can insure the pony against permanent loss of use, veterinary bills, and medical treatment, including dentistry, for the rider. Specified items of tack can also be covered.

Before filling in the form and despatching the first premium, read the small print very carefully and check exclusion clauses. Loss or injury caused through civil riot or war are usually excluded. Acts of God (lightning, tempest or flood) are not. You may find that the policy lists excess amounts which the proposer must pay before final settlement by the insurers. These 'excesses' may range from £5 to £100 depending on the policy and the company.

Ponies over a certain age may be excluded altogether or may attract a very high premium. In some cases, a veterinary examination is required. Twelve or fifteen years old is usually the cut-off age, although most companies will continue insurance cover on an ageing horse which had previously been insured by them.

Under certain conditions, premiums may be reduced: such as for freeze-marking, a lady owner/rider, or Pony Club membership. Some companies operate a no-claims bonus scheme.

The legal responsibilities of the owner are varied. For example, it is up to the owner to prevent the pony from straying. Fences and gates, therefore, should be secure. If a gate is left open or if the pony finds a weak spot in the fence and scrambles through, any damage he causes during the time he is at large should be put right at the owner's expense. Usually, no more harm is done than the worry and inconvenience of having to find and take the pony home and to repair the fence or gate, but if the animal wanders into a neighbouring garden and cuts up the tennis court or destroys the vegetable patch, the repairs could be costly.

The only variation from this is if the pony strays from the highway which he is legally using or from unfenced common land.

Generally speaking, the law seeks to be reasonable. The owner of a pony which has never bitten or kicked anyone would not necessarily be liable if he suddenly acted out of character, although, should this happen a second time, the owner could no longer plead ignorance. Nor could liability necessarily be proved if the pony were teased or provoked into retaliation.

The owner must be particularly careful if a public footpath passes through the pony's field or alongside the fence. A bad-tempered pony who bit someone over the fence, without provocation, could land the owner in trouble. But this could be mitigated if a notice was posted prominently on the footpath warning the public that the pony bites, especially if it could be proved that the notice had been ignored and the injured person had been giving the pony titbits.

Claims arising out of accidents which are not due to negligence on the owner's part – a child falling off and breaking her arm, for example – would be covered under the personal liability clause of the owner's insurance. Even where negligence could be proved, compensation could still be payable under the policy.

The important point to remember is that ownership of a pony carries with it responsibilities which any first-time pony buyer must be prepared to undertake. These cover responsibilities towards other people as well as for the pony's welfare. Most pony-owners think that they are well worthwhile.

Index

Page numbers *in italics* indicate illustration

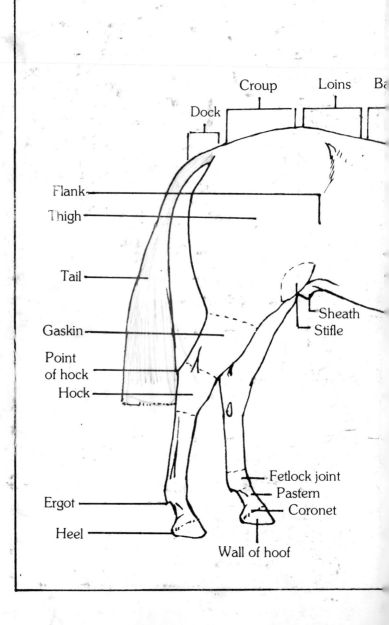

Croup

Loins

Ba

Dock

Flank

Thigh

Tail

Gaskin

Point
of hock

Hock

Ergot

Heel

Sheath
Stifle

Fetlock joint
Pastern
Coronet

Wall of hoof